THE HISTORY OF MINING

BY RYAN GALE

Core Library
An Imprint of Abdo Publishing
abdobooks.com

Cover image: Coal miners use an automatic conveyor. Conveyor belts were first used in coal mining in 1905.

abdobooks.com

Published by Abdo Publishing, a division of ABDO, PO Box 398166, Minneapolis, Minnesota 55439.

Printed in the United States of America, North Mankato, Minnesota.
052023
092023

Cover Photo: George Rinhart/Corbis Historical/Getty Images
Interior Photos: Lewis Hine/Library of Congress/Interim Archives/Archive Photos/Getty Images, 4–5, 43; Glasshouse Images/Alamy, 8; Gary S. Chapman/Photographer's Choice RF/Getty Images, 10–11; Universal History Archive/Universal Images Group/Getty Images, 13, 36, 45; Historica Graphica Collection/Heritage Images/Hulton Archive/Getty Images, 15; North Wind Picture Archives/AP Images, 17; Jon G. Fuller/VWPics/Universal Images Group/Getty Images, 21; 4X5 Collection/Devaney Collection/SuperStock, 22–23; Herbert/Archive Photos/Getty Images, 24; Lewis Wickes Hine/National Child Labor Committee Collection/Library of Congress, 27; The Print Collector/Hulton Archive/Getty Images, 28; Red Line Editorial, 31, 39 (top right); GHI/Universal History Archive/Universal Images Group/Getty Images, 34–35; Shutterstock Images, 39 (top left, bottom left); Blue Ring Media/Shutterstock Images, 39 (bottom right); Mary Altaffer/AP Images 40

Editor: Angela Lim
Series Designer: Ryan Gale

Library of Congress Control Number: 2022949112

Publisher's Cataloging-in-Publication Data
Names: Gale, Ryan, author.
Title: The history of mining / by Ryan Gale
Description: Minneapolis, Minnesota: Abdo Publishing Company, 2024 | Series: Mining in America | Includes online resources and index.
Identifiers: ISBN 9781098290931 (lib. bdg.) | ISBN 9781098277116 (ebook)
Subjects: LCSH: Mines and mining--Juvenile literature. | Mines and mineral resources--Juvenile literature. | American history--Juvenile literature. | Mining engineering--Juvenile literature. | United States--Juvenile literature.
Classification: DDC 622.0973--dc23

CONTENTS

CHAPTER ONE

WORKING UNDERGROUND

George Williams was a miner in the 1870s. He worked at the Clover Hill coal mine in Virginia. The mine had a deep shaft that led from the surface to several long tunnels. Small chambers were carved into the sides of the tunnels. Williams entered one of the chambers. A curtain hung across the entrance to keep coal dust from escaping into the tunnel. He didn't want the floating dust to become a fire hazard.

Miners used mules to help carry coal to the surface in the early 1900s.

Williams used a pickax to break off coal. The chamber was only 5 feet (1.5 m) tall. Williams couldn't stand up straight. He shoveled loose coal and rocks into a mining cart. Once the cart was full, a mule pulled it out of the tunnel. Williams's son worked in the mine as a mule driver. His son was only 14 years old. He was one of many young people working in the mine.

Williams knew mining was dangerous work. Mine tunnels sometimes collapsed. There were other dangers as well. Miners could strike pockets of gas

COAL

Coal is a black rock. It is formed from dead plants that have been compressed over millions of years. Coal is mostly made of the element carbon. It gives off energy in the form of heat when burned, which makes it a great fuel. The more carbon coal contains, the more heat it gives off. Anthracite, or hard coal, is 86 to 97 percent carbon. Bituminous coal, or soft coal, is 45 to 86 percent carbon. Coal is a cheap and widely available fuel. But burning coal emits carbon dioxide and other gases that contribute to climate change.

trapped underground. Williams's steel pickax sometimes created sparks when it hit rocks. The sparks could ignite the gas. They could also cause the coal dust that floated in the air to explode. Sixty-nine people had been killed recently when the nearby Bright Hope mine exploded.

PERSPECTIVES

LIFE IN A COAL MINE

G. W. Weippiert was a journalist in 1892. He toured an Iowa coal mine that year and wrote about his experience. His article was featured in newspapers across the United States. It gave people a glimpse into the daily life of a coal miner. Weippiert wrote in the article: "To earn $1.50 a day, a miner must labor . . . ten hours a day amid surroundings that would strike terror to the heart of the ordinary citizen."

Coal mining was also unhealthy. Williams inhaled coal dust every day. Over time, it became hard for him to breathe. Williams needed the money from coal mining to support his family. People also needed coal to heat their homes and businesses. Coal powered steam engines on trains

Wives of coal miners were often responsible for childcare and house chores.

and ships. It fueled furnaces and forges in the iron, steel, and glass industries.

Miners sometimes worked ten hours or more a day. They worked six days a week. Most of the miners lived in a nearby town that had been built by the Clover Hill Mining Company. Williams rented a small two-room house there. The rent was high. But there was nowhere else to live near the mine. His wife, Mary, worked in the town washing clothes for the miners. Mary also gave medical care to sick and injured miners. Sometimes she cleaned the home of the mine owner for additional income. The mine owner made far more money than the miners. His house was much bigger and nicer than the other houses in town.

A COMMON STORY

Between the 1860s and early 1900s, mining families across the United States had similar experiences to the Williams family. But new technology helped make mining jobs easier. Machines replaced hand tools. Vehicles allowed materials to be moved faster. Labor laws also helped miners get paid more, work fewer hours, and stay healthier.

Miners endured dangerous work sites and poor living conditions. Sometimes they had to fight for improvements. The daily life of miners is just one aspect of the fascinating history of mining in the United States.

EXPLORE ONLINE

Chapter One talks about health problems caused by coal dust. The website below talks more about the subject. Does the website answer any questions you have about coal dust and health?

MINING HEALTH SAFETY

abdocorelibrary.com/history-of-mining

EARLY MINING IN AMERICA

Mining in the United States began around 9,500 years ago in the western Great Lakes region. This region still contains the world's largest copper deposits today. Copper typically forms as an ore. Ores are rocks or minerals that contain small amounts of metal. The metal has to be separated from the other materials before it can be used. But copper in the western Great Lakes region formed as a pure metal, called native copper. Native copper can be used right

American Indians in the United States mined flint. They shaped the material into tools, such as arrowheads.

out of the ground. Ancient American Indians dug up copper nuggets. They used stone hammers to flatten the nuggets. They used copper to make objects like arrowheads, axes, and jewelry.

Ancient American Indians mined other materials as well. Some mined flint to make arrowheads and knives. The ancient Anasazi people mined turquoise in what is now the southwestern United States. They used it to make jewelry and ceremonial objects. The Hopi are another nation in this region. They mined coal as early as the 1200s. They used it as a heat source.

MINING IN COLONIAL AMERICA

The first English colonists arrived in what is now Virginia in 1606. They arrived to establish a settlement. But they also came in search of valuable minerals like gold, silver, and iron. This was known as prospecting. In 1608 the colonists found iron ore and began shipping it to England. There the ore was melted to separate the iron from other materials. This process is known as smelting.

Blacksmiths shaped mined materials into products such as horseshoes.

The colonists began smelting their own ore soon after. But it wasn't until the 1760s that colonists mined and smelted iron ore in large quantities.

The colonists began mining coal in the early 1700s. Blacksmiths first used coal to heat iron so that the metal could be shaped into tools and other objects. Over time, people began using coal to heat their homes.

Miners in colonial America used steel mining picks to break off iron and coal in mines and quarries.

Miners then used shovels to transfer the loose ores into wheelbarrows. In large mines, horses pulled mining carts. Once aboveground, the material was loaded onto wagons for transport to towns or cities.

By the time of the Revolutionary War (1775–1783), the combined iron output of the 13 colonies was among the largest in the world. The United States formed after winning the war and grew rapidly. Demand for iron and steel goods increased, and mining expanded to meet the demand. As coal mining increased between the 1820s and 1860s, more people began to use coal instead of wood for heating and cooking in their households.

UNIONS

Mining was dangerous work. Miners were injured and killed by falling debris. And they often inhaled dust that damaged their lungs. Mining also paid little. Miners in Pennsylvania fought for better pay in 1848. They formed one of the first mining unions in the United States.

Coal miners in Pennsylvania went on strike in 1902, resulting in a coal shortage. People lined the streets to receive coal to heat their homes.

A union is an organization made up of workers. They work as a group to fight for better pay and safer working conditions.

At first the miners' employer refused to pay the miners more. So the miners went on strike. A strike is a form of protest. Employees stop working during a strike. This causes employers to lose money. Employers may give the strikers what they want so the employees will return to work. The Pennsylvania strike lasted three weeks. It convinced the employer to pay the miners more money.

More miners formed unions, and eventually the American Miners' Association was created in 1861. It was the first national miners' union. It accepted miners from across the United States.

THE CALIFORNIA GOLD RUSH

Gold was discovered in California in 1848. Word of the discovery spread quickly. People began pouring into the region in 1849. They were known as the forty-niners. By the mid-1850s, as many as 300,000 people had come to California. It was one of the largest migrations of people in US history. The period was called the California Gold Rush.

Gold seekers saw land in California as free to claim. Miners placed wooden stakes around the land

Approximately $2 billion of gold was mined during the California Gold Rush, but few prospectors became rich.

they wanted. This was called staking a claim. It did not give people legal rights to the land. Some gold miners trespassed on other peoples' claims and tried to steal the land claims of others. There were no laws governing the region, so many disputes led to violence.

Gold in California was often located near the surface. Many people used metal pans to mine for gold. They put surface dirt in the pans and added water. They swirled the water in the pans so the lightweight dirt spilled out, revealing the heavier gold. This was called panning,

THE COMSTOCK LODE

The California Gold Rush wasn't the only mining rush in US history. The discovery of a large vein, or lode, of silver by several miners near Virginia City, Nevada, triggered a silver rush in 1859. The silver lode was named after Henry Comstock, one of the people who made the discovery. Thousands of people headed to western Nevada in search of silver. Silver continued to be extracted from the Comstock Lode into the 1940s.

or placer mining. Panning was a cheap and easy method to find gold. But it was slow and tiring. Some miners built wooden troughs, or sluices, that used flowing water to separate dirt and gold. This method was called sluice mining. It required less work than panning.

Once the surface gold in California was exhausted, some people turned to underground mining. They dug mines and used chisels and

PERSPECTIVES

AMERICAN INDIANS AND THE GOLD RUSH

Many white Americans who traveled to California during the gold rush passed through traditional American Indian hunting grounds. They overhunted animal populations that American Indians relied on for food. Miners took over American Indian lands. They killed and enslaved American Indian men, women, and children. Historian Natasha Stange studied the effects of the gold rush on American Indians. She wrote in a 2021 article: "The massive migration of white miners caused by the gold rush permanently disrupted the lifestyles and local economies of countless Indian tribes across the American West."

explosives to break apart rocks. Some miners used horses and mules to pull mining carts. But underground mining was not an option for everyone. Most people could not afford the necessary equipment and animals. And not everyone was willing to risk the dangers of cave-ins.

TENT CITIES AND BOOMTOWNS

The thousands of miners who took part in the California Gold Rush needed somewhere to live. Some lived in cloth tents. Large collections of tents were called tent cities. Merchants in tent cities sold food and equipment to miners. Tent cities also had bathhouses, restaurants, and churches.

Over time, tents gave way to sturdier structures made of wood. Mining towns grew so quickly people called them boomtowns. Like other towns throughout the United States, boomtowns had stores, hotels, restaurants, and theaters. But when mines ran out of gold, people left mining towns as quickly as they

The Goldfield Ghost Town is a reconstruction of the Mammoth gold mining town in Arizona that was established in the 1890s.

had arrived. Buildings, wagons, and equipment were abandoned. People call the abandoned towns ghost towns. Some are still standing today and offer a unique glimpse of the past.

FURTHER EVIDENCE

Chapter Two discusses the early history of mining in America. What was one of the main points of the chapter? What are some pieces of evidence used to support that point? Read the article at the website below. Does the information on the website support the main point of the chapter? Does it present new information?

OLD COPPER CULTURE

abdocorelibrary.com/history-of-mining

CHAPTER THREE

A MINING REVOLUTION

Mining in America skyrocketed during the Second Industrial Revolution (1870–1914). This period saw rapid growth in technology and mass production. It led to a major expansion of railroads and the creation of skyscrapers and automobiles. The growth of cities and transportation required large amounts of steel. Huge quantities of coal were needed to

The steam shovel was developed during the Second Industrial Revolution. It greatly increased the amount of mined materials that miners could extract each day.

Miners placed explosives, such as dynamite, to break open rocks and access ores.

heat homes and provide fuel for forges and electricity. Mining increased to meet the rising demand.

The steam engine was one of the most important innovations during the Second Industrial Revolution. Steam engines turned water into steam, which could be used to power machines. These engines ran pumps that removed water from mines. They powered elevators that moved people and equipment into and out of mines. They also were used in large steam shovels that could dig more than 1,000 tons (900 metric tons) of materials a day. Steam-powered trains and ships allowed vast amounts of iron ore and coal to be quickly transported.

Pneumatic tools were another innovation. They used compressed air to make mechanical parts move. Miners used pneumatic picks to excavate ores. They used pneumatic drills to make holes in solid rock. Pneumatic tools quickly replaced hand picks and drills.

BIG BUSINESS

Some mining businesses grew into large companies during the Second Industrial Revolution. They were able to buy out smaller companies. Large companies had the money to hire many workers, build numerous mines, and buy the latest mining technology.

The General Mining Law of 1872 allowed miners and mining companies to stake claims on government land that had mineral deposits on it. It was meant to promote development of public land. Mining companies used the law to build iron, copper, and coal mines across the United States.

MINE WORKERS

The mining industry required thousands of miners. In the 1880s mine owners began hiring immigrants from Europe, Canada, Central and South America, and China. Some immigrant miners were willing to work for less money than US miners.

Underground miners were not the only workers in the mining industry. Other workers separated the ore and coal from useless rock. Some people loaded the pure materials onto trains and ships. Workers operated and fixed machinery. Bosses, or foremen, managed the mines and workers.

Women also worked in the mining industry. Social expectations and state laws prevented them from working in the mines. They were restricted to working in mining towns as cooks, teachers, and nurses. Most were wives or relatives of male workers.

Children worked in the mining industry as well. Some worked in mining towns, but others as young as ten worked in the mines. Many worked as trappers.

A young trapper boy waited by the door in a West Virginia mine to let mine cars pass through in 1908.

They opened and closed doors that allowed mining carts to pass from one section of a mine to another. Children also worked sorting coal from stone. Child labor laws were passed in the late 1800s and early 1900s. They prevented companies from exploiting child workers. State laws set the minimum age for child workers. And some permitted children to work only after school and on vacation days.

COMPANY TOWNS

Some mining companies built their own towns to house their workers. Company towns had houses that

Many buildings stood along Main Street in Butte, Montana, a copper boomtown in the late 1800s.

workers rented. Many towns had hospitals, schools, and churches. Most had general stores that sold food and clothing. Miners couldn't always afford to buy goods at company stores. Some stores issued miners credit in the form of scrip. This was money that could be used only at company stores. Once used, the scrip's value was deducted from the miners' paychecks.

Companies sometimes threatened to evict, or remove, miners from their homes if they quit or went on strike. Company towns declined between the 1920s and 1930s. This was due to the wider availability of public transportation and automobiles, which allowed miners to live off site and ride or drive to work.

DEMANDING MORE

Mining was a dangerous job. By 1900, one person died for every 100,000 tons (90,720 metric tons) of coal mined. At least 361 miners died when a large explosion rocked the Monongah Mine in West Virginia on December 6, 1907. It was the worst mining disaster in US history. The US Bureau of Mines was created in 1910 as a result. This federal agency investigated mining disasters and researched ways to prevent them.

Miners wanted to be safe at work. They wanted mining companies to cover hospital bills if they were injured on the job. Miners also wanted to be paid more money and to work fewer hours. Some miners protested against poor conditions by going on strike.

Mining companies dealt with strikes in several ways. Company officials often negotiated with strikers so that each side could get something they wanted. But some

PERSPECTIVES

MOTHER JONES

Mary Harris Jones was an activist. She fought for workers' rights in the late 1800s and early 1900s. She organized strikes and convinced miners to join unions. The people she helped saw her as a mother figure. They called her Mother Jones. Historian Elliott Gorn wrote about Mother Jones in 2001. He said, "She organized workers, women, and minorities, drawing public attention to their hardships and giving them a voice."

companies replaced workers that went on strike. Some hired strikebreakers, who often tried to end strikes using violence.

West Virginia saw a series of violent clashes between 1912 and 1921. It came to be known as the West Virginia Mine Wars. The conflict came to a climax in August 1921. A group of 10,000 protesting miners marched across southern West Virginia. They were stopped by a large group of lawmen at Blair Mountain. Several people were killed and wounded. It came to be known as the Battle of Blair Mountain.

COAL MINING DEATHS

The United States has a long history of coal mining. What do you notice about the changes in the number of coal miners and coal mining deaths in US history? How is this related to changing technologies and mining laws?

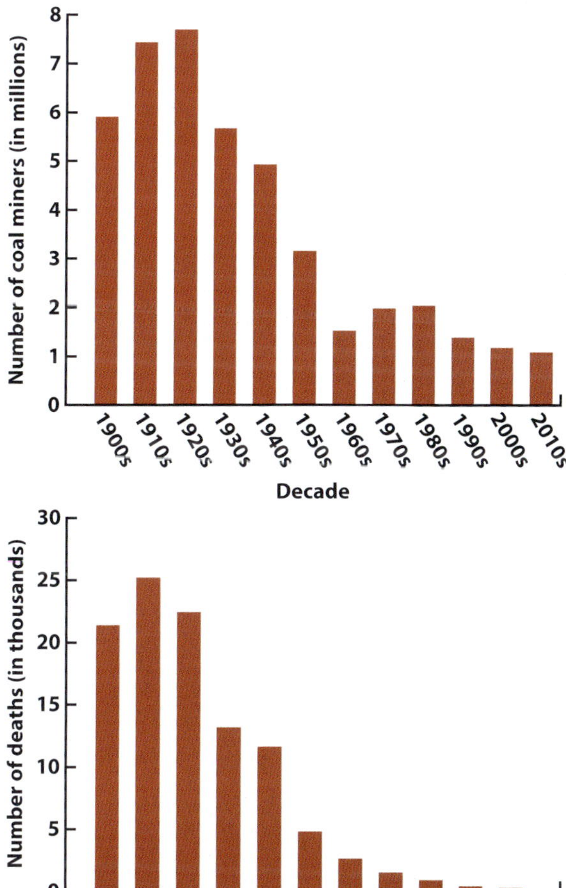

THE COAL AND IRON POLICE

Mining companies in Pennsylvania wanted their own security force in the 1860s. Local police forces were not able to effectively guard mines and protect mining towns. So the state allowed the mining industry to create its own police force in 1866. It was called the Coal and Iron Police. But mining companies also used their police forces to break up union meetings and strikes. The Coal and Iron Police arrested and beat miners to end strikes. Some miners made reports to the state government. They said the Coal and Iron Police were breaking the law. As a result, the governor abolished the Coal and Iron Police in 1931.

Labor movements during the Second Industrial Revolution bore results in the 1930s and 1940s. Working and living conditions began to improve. The government passed mining safety laws. It also passed minimum wage laws.

STRAIGHT TO THE SOURCE

A reporter for Louisiana's *Opelousas Courier* visited a coal mine in 1900. Afterward, he commented on the mining industry:

> *The life of a coal miner has improved vastly of recent years. Many of the features that used to shorten his life and make it one of extreme hazard has been eliminated, or at least vastly reduced in danger. . . . But with all these new safeguards the life is not an [appealing] one. The pay is small, the work is hard, and the dangers still many. The only really pleasant way to be connected with a coal mine is as the owner of one.*

Source: "Life in a Coal Mine." *Opelousas Courier*, 10 Feb. 1900, p. 3.

WHAT'S THE BIG IDEA?

Read the primary source text carefully. What is its main idea? Explain how the main idea is supported by details. List two or three of those supporting details.

CHAPTER FOUR

A STRUGGLING INDUSTRY

The mining industry has had many ups and downs. Major events like wars and economic depressions affected the industry. The prices of steel and coal dropped significantly during the Great Depression (1929–1941). Building projects across the United States ground to a halt, and mines closed as a result. Thousands of miners lost their jobs.

The need for mined materials increased again during World War II (1939–1945).

A miner loaded mercury into a mine car in 1942. This metal was used to make military equipment, such as bomb detonators, for World War II.

Copper was one of the mined materials that was in high demand during World War II. Train cars full of copper ore arrived in Salt Lake County in Utah in 1942.

Steel, copper, and lead were needed in great quantities during the war. They were used to make ships, airplanes, and ammunition.

FEMALE MINERS

Thousands of men joined the armed forces during World War II, which left a large gap in the mining workforce. Women stepped in to fill the gap. Some state laws and mining unions prohibited women from doing dangerous jobs, such as digging in mines. So women were employed to separate minerals from rock, repair machinery, and drive trucks.

These women had to give up their jobs when the war ended. Their jobs went to men returning from the war. There were no laws that protected the rights of women in the workplace. But that began to change in the 1960s. The government passed laws that banned employers from making hiring decisions based on gender.

PERSPECTIVES

COAL AND BAYONETS

A coal miner strike threatened to stop coal production in the spring of 1943. The country was fighting in World War II at the time, and coal was essential to the war effort. The government threatened to use the military to end the strike. Miners rallied together saying, "You can't dig coal with bayonets." A bayonet is a blade placed at the end of a military rifle. On May 1, President Franklin D. Roosevelt placed US coal mines under government control. Eventually, the federal government listened to the miners' demands.

THE DECLINE OF COAL

Coal use began to decline in the United States in

the 1970s. The cost of other fuels such as oil and natural gas began to decrease. These fuels started to compete with coal. Scientists researched the effects burning coal had on the environment and people's health. Coal releases carbon dioxide when burned. This contributes to climate change. It also releases sulfur dioxide, which can cause breathing problems. This research led to further declines in coal use. Coal mines closed, and thousands of miners were out of work.

New technologies also affected the mining industry. The continuous miner and other digging machines

TACONITE

Mines in Minnesota's Mesabi Iron Range produced hundreds of thousands of tons of iron ore during World War II. But the region's high-grade ore was exhausted soon after. High-grade ore is more than 50 percent iron. Miners turned to taconite as an alternative. Taconite is a type of low-quality iron ore. It is only 20 to 30 percent iron. When high-grade ore was plentiful, taconite was discarded as a waste product. Afterward, it helped save Minnesota's mining industry.

COMPARING MINING TOOLS

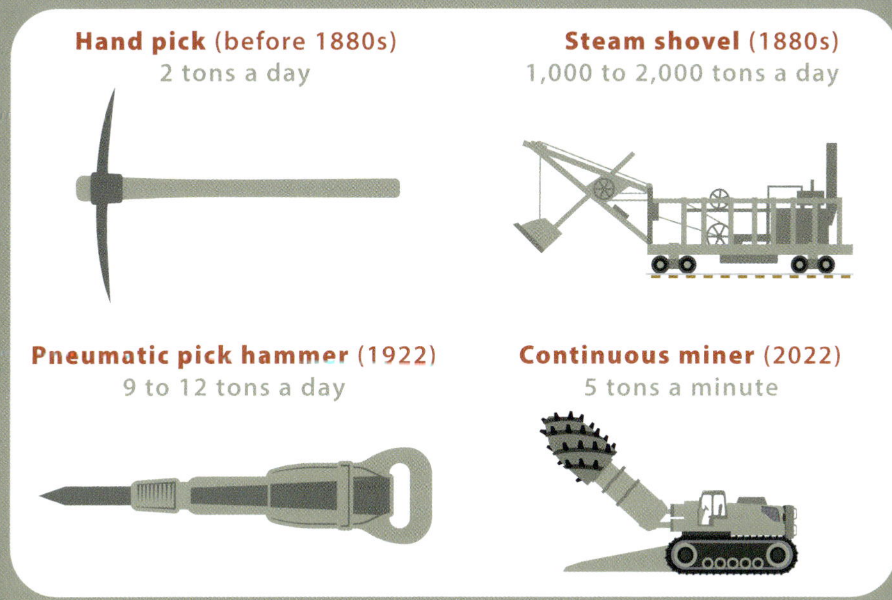

Many tools have been used throughout mining history. What types of tools are able to extract the most materials in a day? How do you think these tools will improve in the future?

could mine approximately 5 tons (4.5 metric tons) of coal a minute. Conveyor belts could carry ores to the surface at high speeds. Fewer miners were required.

VIEWS ON MINING

Mining is an important topic of discussion today. Many people see mining as necessary to help the nation succeed. Iron ore is needed to make steel for building

Miners and supporters of mine workers demonstrated in New York in 2021. They called attention to the need for fair wages and better employment practices.

projects, and coal is used to provide electricity for homes and businesses. Rare earth metals are used to make computer chips and batteries. Mining also creates thousands of jobs and helps the economy.

But mining vehicles and processing plants pollute the air. Mining waste can pollute drinking water. Mines also destroy animal habitats. Mines are sometimes abandoned with little or no cleanup. They can continue polluting the environment even when they are no longer in use. Many people have formed negative opinions about mining because of these issues. Some people fight to stop mining. But mining has played a major role in US history and still plays an important role today.

STRAIGHT TO THE SOURCE

Mining creates new jobs, but it can also harm the environment. Reporter April Dembosky wrote about a proposed mine in Alaska in 2006:

> *When mining projects attract criticism from environmental activists, their most reliable defense has always been the thousands of jobs the company will provide to an otherwise economically depressed community. . . . But numerous locals and advocacy groups have complained that the potential environmental damage far outweighs any [positives]: toxic mining chemicals, they say, might seep into sensitive salmon spawning streams; transport roads will cut through pristine Alaskan wilderness; noise of heavy machinery and vehicles will disrupt caribou and moose migration.*

Source: April Dembosky. "On the Cultural Impacts of Mining." *Mother Jones*, 7 June 2006, motherjones.com. Accessed 10 Oct. 2022.

POINT OF VIEW

The writer of this article describes the environmental impact of mines. What is the writer's view of opening new mines? Read back through this chapter. Do you agree with the writer's points? Why or why not?

FAST FACTS

- American Indians began mining copper around 9,500 years ago in the western Great Lakes region.
- As many as 300,000 people traveled to California during the gold rush in 1849. It was one of the largest migrations of people in US history.
- Miners in Pennsylvania formed one of the first mining unions in the United States in 1848.
- New mining technology, such as the steam shovel, increased mining production during the Second Industrial Revolution.
- The General Mining Law of 1872 allowed individuals and companies to prospect and mine on land owned by the government.
- Some mining companies built towns near their mines for their workers to live in.
- Miners in Pennsylvania formed one of the first mining unions in the United States in 1848. They fought for better pay.
- Mining companies hired thousands of women during World War II to replace men who had joined the military. But most lost their jobs when the war ended.

- Coal mining began to decline in the 1970s when other fuels like natural gas and oil became cheaper.
- Public opinion on mining today is influenced by the industry's impact on the environment.

STOP AND THINK

Take a Stand

When building new mines, it is important to consider the environmental impact as well as the economic benefit. Imagine that a mining company wants to build a new mine in an undeveloped area. Are the jobs the mine will create worth potentially harming the environment? Write a short essay outlining your stance on the issue. Make sure you explain your opinion and your reasons for it. Include facts and details that support your reasons.

Another View

This book talks about women working in the mining industry. As you know, every source is different. Ask a librarian or another adult to help you find another source about this topic. Write a short essay comparing and contrasting your source's point of view with that of this book's author. What is the point of view of each author? How are they similar and why? How are they different and why?

Tell the Tale

Chapter One of this book discusses the daily life of a miner in the 1870s. Imagine you are working as a miner during that time. Write 200 words about the difficulties you experience as a miner. How could you make the mine a less dangerous place to work?

Surprise Me

Chapter Two discusses the California Gold Rush. After reading this chapter, what two or three facts about the gold rush did you find most surprising? Write a few sentences about each fact. Why did you find each fact surprising?

GLOSSARY

advocacy
public support for a cause, idea, or plan

climate change
the long-term change in weather patterns

compress
to press or squeeze together

deposit
a natural source of a mineral, metal, or ore

depression
a lengthy downturn in the economy

forge
a workshop where metal is heated and shaped

innovation
a new invention or device

mineral
a naturally occurring material that is typically found underground

mule
the offspring of a female horse and a male donkey

pneumatic
operated by air

quarry
an open-air pit where stone, coal, or other material is mined

ONLINE RESOURCES

To learn more about the history of mining, visit our free resource websites below.

Visit **abdocorelibrary.com** or scan this QR code for free Common Core resources for teachers and students, including vetted activities, multimedia, and booklinks, for deeper subject comprehension.

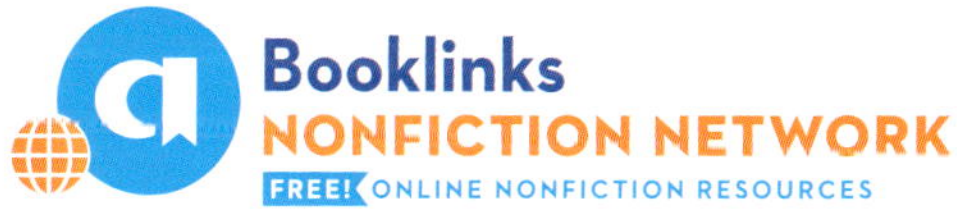

Visit **abdobooklinks.com** or scan this QR code for free additional online weblinks for further learning. These links are routinely monitored and updated to provide the most current information available.

LEARN MORE

Eboch, Chris. *Rocks and Minerals: Get the Dirt on Geology.* Nomad, 2020.

Kaiser, Emma. *Mining and the Environment*. Abdo, 2024.

INDEX

About the Author

Ryan Gale is an artist and writer from Minnesota. Having grown up in a mining town, he has always been interested in the history of mining.